The Singing Hollow

By the same author:
Thames Way (2015)
A Thousand Sparks (2018)

The Singing Hollow

a collection of poems

Diarmuid Fitzgerald

Alba Publishing

Published by Alba Publishing,
P O Box 266, Uxbridge
UB9 5NX, United Kingdom
www.albapublishing.com

A catalogue record for this book is available from the British Library

ISBN: 978-1-912773-43-5

Edited, designed and typeset by Kim Richardson
Cover photo © Estate of Paul Henry / IVARO, Dublin 2022,
courtesy of Whyte's Auctioneers

Printed and bound by Essentra

10 9 8 7 6 5 4 3 2

To the members of the Parnell Square Writers' Group:
Nessa Collinge, Arlene Fox, Emmaleene O'Brien,
Liz O'Neill, Colin Scuffins

Contents

Part I: The Singing Hollow

Part I: The Singing Hollow

A Different Door
for Daniel Crowley

The shed smelled of paint and dust
as I pushed open the old cracking door.
My grandad stooped over the table
absorbed in his work. I knew to stay silent,
entranced by his moving arms and jerking legs.
I was in awe at the strange things he kept,
tools whose purposes I could not guess.
His knobbly hands with reddened thumbs
could fashion the leg of a chair
from a plank of wood, repair fishing tackle,
or mend the bow on a broken boat.
He sang songs in a worn-out tune.

The shed door is new. Oilskins are gone,
coils rust, the fishing tackle has not been moved
for years and the place is clean.
Light shimmers into all the corners
as shadows are banished and the walls are cold.
No breath heats the windowpane,
the place empty of his touch and craft.

Mowing

for Seamus Fitzgerald

He points with a cane and I move, turn corners more
sharply, reverse, and change my direction.
I pretend I do not know how to mow.

I cut into the heart of the lawn. The blade rotates madly,
keen to do its work. The mower meets a steep gradient,
struggles, chugs, spurts, then spits out wet grass.

He is itching to get behind the wheel. I let my dad
take over. He enjoys the pungent smell of petrol
and the first hint of summer coming in early March.

Driftwood

He sees a ram's head in the way
two branches serve as horns,
gouges in the bole are eyes.
A tree stump is a Medusa's head.
The reek of salt is as sharp as words not said.

A cold draught comes through a half-open shed door.
He spends hours in there, days really, washing the sand off,
paring away the awkward sinews to define something.
Varnish soothes the wood hurt with cuts.

He is alone at the market stall,
crushes gravel with his foot to pass the time.
The torrential rain glazes his woodwork.

Gardening
for Mary Fitzgerald

My mum showed me how to move a juniper shrub
across her garden. She dug the soil with a fork, pulled,
pushed, and shoved. The roots cracked under the effort.
She explained how to take enough soil so the bush
can survive as I plopped it into the wheelbarrow
and wheeled the juniper across the verdant grass,
wet with yesterday's rain.

In my own place, my mum helped me to clear
the back garden. The unkept heather looked forlorn.
We poured salt in between the cracks of the tiles.
Ants scurried about, crazy with anger
as their colony was disturbed. She wrote out
how to remove them and let bees
do their work.

On my own, I work out how to cut the stem
of the ivy to kill it off, deadhead roses
the right way, add mulch to the beds, weed the garden,
sweep the backyard. In moments of confusion
I remember what she said: "If they trouble you,
make sure you dig down deep and clear them
for more to grow."

Bright Morning
for Iona and Ailsa Fitzgerald

In the cold wind,
clouds let rain fall down on the streets.
Weeds crack through the rigorous pavements
and mist dissolves. Dewdrops congregate on windows.

Your eyes rotate behind closed eyelids,
nerves tingle and your legs
stretch out for your first steps.
Keep on going by focusing on your breath.

Naked trees will come back to life,
leaves coaxed out by the promise of fresh air.
A root searches in its slow way
for something to grasp.

The Feather Hair Clip

I am on the balcony. On the stage
below a young woman wears
a feather hair clip. Her black hair
is pulled through like sand running in an hourglass.
 A gleam moves up and down the clip as her head
moves. She picks up her bow, plays the violin.
The cello weeps slowly and the clarinet airs lightly.
She sways her body to the music and I sway
my body in rhythm with hers. She does not
see me looking at her. I catch a glimpse of her face
after the melody fades into silence.

The Red Line Tram

On the way home
a father and his little girl stand.
He has just enough room to kneel down
to take out from their buggy

a tray of sushi and turn around to her.
He opens it and picks out one roll,
with green seaweed, rice, and pink ginger.
He places it delicately into her mouth.

She eats it without a slurp,
this slow ceremony keeps going
despite the juddering of the tram
and the passengers slipping out.

He takes out a bottle of water
and lets its coolness flow down her throat.
The water sloshes up the bottle,
then he wipes her lips with his finger.

The tram picks up speed
and the buggy moves untethered,
bumps into various obstacles
and rolls further out of reach.

Aftermath

They knife their food in unison, scrape their plates.
She clears her throat and asks for the salt.
A hard word from him falls onto the table.

He marches out around the garden,
pulls leaves off the shrubs,
tests the hose, checks the lawnmower.

She pokes the fire. Feeds kindling to the flames.
Runs her finger down the tongs,
tension held in the clasped claws.

Pass

The air is clenched tight. Embers spark
from the fireplace. We speak in staccato tones.
An anvil of guilt sits in my stomach
after last night's crossing of words.

For space and time, I drive to Connor Pass.
Fog clouds the road, rendering
my map useless. A stream runs furiously
from Peddler's Lake, slapping the cliff.

I return home and let the silence
soothe out an apology. You still read
the newspaper, turn it sharply. In my pocket
a compass twirls and twirls in frenzy.

Lady of the Lake

(inspired by the work of art Muse *by Laura Christensen)*

she lives on a boat
in a pool of her own tears
and shimmers like glass
the water floods the boat

she puts her foot into a coiled rope
attached to a piano
going down
into the bottom of the lake

her hooped dress billows over her face
dull as deep-sea calm
the skin of the water hides
the torrents of her tears

Departure
(inspired by the painting Parc en Aer *by Wendy Dison)*

for Margaret Fitzgerald

The Singer sewing machine
was on the kitchen table.
Flames licked at the stove lid
as a pot of potatoes boiled.

She paused to look at the weather,
adjust the radio crackle. A letter
told her of the birth and death of cousins.
She hid it with her grief in a biscuit tin.

She stitched and restitched the clothes
as this was the only sympathy she had time for.
Her teenage boys worked in the fields
before they were sent out to toughen in the world.

The roof is gone. Air comes through
the windows, pushes soot around the kitchen.
The Singer has seized up and rusts in the backyard.
A bee struggles to find nectar, sets off on a new departure.

The Trees of Kenya
(I.M. Wangari Maathai 1940 - 2011)

The swallows fly from their perch in the oak trees
at my local park. They swirl, turn, dip and swoop
in graceful unison, then fly to Kenya
and wait on an acacia tree over the dry grass.

The companies came to clear the land,
overturn the ground for a quick turnover,
filling the pockets of hungry shareholders,
helped by brown envelopes to politicians.

There were no trees to keep the ground in place.
The rivers ran red from rain-washed soil
like blood from the tribespeople, shot
for speaking up and telling their story.

But not this lady, who burned with passion
in her heart. She spoke over men who felt
they knew better. She waded through trouble
and gathered like-minded ladies.

They planted trees to breathe in carbon
and breathe out fresh air. The roots grew slowly,
held the ground together
like hands forming strong bonds.

The season passes and a whole forest
unfurls again. Bird song starts to fill the air.
The swallows gather once more to murmurate
and fly back to the oaks in my park.

The Dream Tree

(inspired by the painting Cinderella Doesn't Live Here
Anymore *by Barbara Graff)*

The sky is dark with fear.
The moon is a yellow parachute
making shadows long.

Salena is with her two children in the bathroom
before bedtime. Badriya and Amin wash their faces,
a car bomb goes off.

Salena runs, squeezing their hands.
Her shoes stick in the mud
and she abandons them.

They reach a border post. Salena fumbles
for her paperwork and can't find it.
She gives the guard an unspoken favour.

Salena tells Badriya and Amin about the dream tree,
which sways its branches when you sing
and the tree makes your dreams come true.

The moon shines over the campsite.
Badriya and Amin stand with a yellow sheet
between them and trace the outline of their faces.

Invitation

The moon is like a radiant eye.
Shrubs form a silhouetted row and light
scatters through into small pools.

The grass tingles
my folded legs as I feel
an invitation to a silent dance.

I see myself, head bowed, toes
pointed three feet off the ground,
swaying like a loose pendulum.

Repulsed, I run back
into the kitchen. Stalling at the window
I float out, pulsing to her light.

Silent House

On the skylight, a spider sits
and eyes me. It waits,
legs arched and tense.

Electric light pours
through the gap under the door.
A floorboard creaks somewhere.

I check the hallway but it is empty.
Dust moves, a draught flows up the stairs
giving a chill that has no name.

I close the door and sense a presence beyond,
worm-eaten, blue-eyed, with a rotting head.
My mind keeps adding more detail.

I get into bed and hope the sheet will mother me.
I have no stomach, just a black hole
with darkness spilling out.

Night Drive

I set out and the full moon is in the sky.
The road curves suddenly in on itself,
a carpet of black with cat's eyes.

The moonlight silences the sea,
a ring of copper around torn clouds.
A town glitters against the bay
as mud sucks the water in.

My lights flash against another car
which flashes back, momentarily blinding me.
The dial moves up a number
and time stands away.

There is surprise in each corner
and yet the same darkness stays with me,
the same line of paint glowing.
The road unfolds as it does
neither adding nor taking away.
Finally, my mind is quiet.

Way Home

The darkness has merged the street with the sky.
Orange lights block out the stars
and the wind changes the litter on the road.
A fox searches for food from open bins.

Passing houses sharpen as shadows ebb.
Some people nod their heads on the bus,
a few stragglers pick their way home
too drunk to see the dawn light.

I get off the bus from the city centre,
hear the tap my shoes make on the footpath.
The last thing I remember of the night
is the draught going around me as I close the door.

Rented House

As you open the front door
the light through the fan window is lost for a while.

Dampness from mouldy walls wets the window.
A door may be slammed,
keys lost, or an argument had over unpaid bills.
The spark of anger is doused
as you keep your distance.

The shape that you carry from house to house
is a suitcase. The view from various bedrooms
changes over the years.

Through the neighbour's window
a family sits down to a hot meal
and the steam clouds the glass.

A Sort of Song

What can I say but say the same thing
everyone else has said?

The swan and swallow sing of the dying day.
Leaves drop and wither, the river slurps on.
The sun goes down as nature shrugs.

I come home to a room where
I do not hear my family – far, far from
this new land of neon, rush and crowds.

Staying at home all day is very fine
but it will not serve me any good
nor bring a crowd of friends near.

Maybe I can say something in my own way
but if so who will notice my song?

Boundary Mirage

I ease myself out of the house without a word,
give my companions space. I am tired of the same faces
and the same groove of conversations.
I run to propel myself from the task of being useful,
circle that void where days are wasted.

During the run, I imagine cars are abandoned on the street,
electric pylons burn, deer commandeer the local park,
people turn into zombies with eyes fixed on screens.

I come to the kilometre limit, dance on the boundary,
thumb my nose. On the canal towpath, children play
and whole families cycle under the blessed weather.

Back home, I collapse on the sofa, now wishing to see
a familiar face again, and let the silence do the talking.

Bottle Bank Therapy

On the first day of ease from the lockdown, I bring
a box full of bottles, green, brown, clear and blue.
They shine in the sun. Glass shards litter the ground.
I pick my way carefully to the bank and select a bottle.
The neck is smooth. I lob it down the hole,
listen to the cacophony of the breaking,
a joyous crashing sound, the way the glass clinks
through glass, makes the sound of rain. It is heaven
to me as I let go and keep letting go and think how will
we gather our smashed selves into a new whole.

Faltering into Sound

On the balcony a clear plastic hanger
half twirls on a pole, casting a rainbow light
around the room. I plough through the early poems
of faltering grace of a poet

now worthy of great praise.
In hopeful comparison
I try to find my rung
on a ladder of failures and compromises.

In that turning delicacy, I wonder
if I can do more than skim a stone of words
across the surface,
that when I call the language comes.

Like the deep muffle of my breath,
a hemmed skirt ruffling down the stairs,
a drunken man reaching for light.
The slack curtains shield the night's freeze.

Outside the hanger tilts again in the breeze.
I push my hand against a wall
of straining silence
to make an indentation of sound.

The Singing Hollow

Deep in the bowels of Dublin, there is St. Audoen's Park.
In the middle is a singing hollow,
a slab of rock, upright, grey,
with a hole carved into it.
You are invited to place your head inside,
clear your throat, purse your lips, and hum
until all your organs are in tune
and the pulse matches the stone.
Waves spread out and meet
the road, blackbirds, apartments.
All vibrate in concert,
beyond what the ears and eyes can tell
but the heart knows.

Water Table

Red cranes are busy after being slack.
A random gap in the chipboard shows a steep drop
and a corrugated wall holds up the other bank.

Water bleeds through. This hole is no longer
a fresh cut. The city feels its veins,
wants new wounds. Progress is like a thief.

In the mucky pool
water creeps in a slow insinuation,
saliva running down a blocked throat.

Concrete will be poured in and the hole
staunched with glass and steel.
In the mud, nettles multiply and grow rich.

Snowdrift

The walls around our gardens are high.
We keep our distance, reassure each other
that this will all eventually blow over.
Small talk hides our frequent sighs.

The snowdrift shakes over the street
and cars are plastered with a hard frost.
A canopy of trees become torn quilts.
Parents try to catch the flakes.

Children go from garden to garden
increasing the populace with snowmen
and very gradually with snow cover
houses become one common colour.

Settlings

Seaweed is stubborn here
and the dipping waves wash over
a confetti of rusted pebbles and stones.

Who knows what stories these stones can tell?
If I smash them with questions
their shards will remain faithful to silence.

The rain brings thoughts
of my sister to me. I wish I could
clasp her hand with my hand.

The cup of the sky holds my dreams.
I must meet myself kindly
at the frothed high-water line.

On Brighton Beach

Waves lap the stone shore
like a child licking ice cream.
There is a path of cold copper
stretching out under the sun.
The early spring sky is clean blue.
An unleashed Labrador runs by,
its owner a black smut against the horizon.

I stand under the pier,
a tunnel of beams where waves meet
the tinkling music of razzmatazz rides.
Perhaps I shall move here and become
familiar with the pull of the sea.

Up on the pier a boy crouches,
sets a top spinning and watches it
wander from one side to the other.

At The Still Point

The shadows of the oak trees are broken into blobs.
Wind rushes over the surface and pondweed
carpets the lake floor. The ravens go
in their autumnal circles.

I dawdle here a little as my house is empty.
Its walls are my companions. My usual chair
tries to comfort me. The fridge hums
to fill the cool space.

I listen to the waves through the boughs
and I say yes to my worries: a written reprimand
from my stiff boss, a brush-off text from a supposed date,
an unexpected bill arriving at my door.

Then a sudden brightening,
the sun glistening on the pond
and the ripples criss-cross over and over.

The Bridge

The canal is quilted with brown leaves.
There are nine trees on the right bank,
teasing towards nudity. My college days
are over and my friendships are going to break.
I am left with the company of water and trees.
I walk under the bridge and whistle to its stones
not wanting to return to my house.
A large flock of swans sit on the bridge
their underbellies pure white.
Being mute, they keep to their hush
and fly in unison and settle in the rushes
on the other bank, further beyond my reach.

Aughacasla Strand

The wide bay is shaped like a horseshoe.
The sand fills the pools and algae covers
the rocks. The wash comes in then goes out
with a crash. My debts pile up, drag
me down. I lost my job and my world shakes.
I seek to clear my head as it pounds
then run to find an answer, make an imprint
of feet. I release my thoughts into the waves
which pull back, leaving the shingle shining
in rusted browns, yellows, reds and blues.

In Glendalough Wood

The breeze comes through the spruce trees
where the air is filled with peppermint.
Light filters onto a blanket of pins.

I stop on the wooden bridge
where the scented wind blows around.
My head churns with heavy thoughts

as a forest of applications sits on my desk.
I am here seeking a way out
and see the tree trunks blocking my path.

I drop my bag, relax my shoulders,
and dip my hand into the stream
and know the flow finds its own way.

Clouds on Caherconree

The tops of the mountains
are covered in a thick white
with hints of grey on the underside.
Caherconree looks like a forehead against the sea,
slowly carved by ice, wind, and water over eons.
Rivers run down like worry lines.
These clouds are getting fat.
They soak up trouble until a thunderclap comes,
a drum banged, and rain falls slantways
and urgent, jumping from object to object,
dancing to replenish the rivers
and keep the Earth in flow.

Part II: Camino Cantos

Hymn

a steeple appearing over a hill
a rose hip bud in this early spring
a sudden opening in the hedgerow
a breeze blowing dirt from the path
a click-clack sound from walking poles
a sunbeam breaking through the clouds
a green field that seems to go on and on
a leaf from an olive tree brushing the wind
a sharp turn in the path as it zig-zags down a slope

Silent Town

The town on the hill keeps moving away
no matter how close I seem to get.
I am sore with worries and these legs.

The April wind changes swiftly from hot to cold.
I take off my rucksack ten times
yet it is heavier each time, despite having no water.

The road turns and quickly I arrive.
Sheets of wood lie against front doors.
No child kicks a football. Dirt and dead wind.

The silence of this town reminds me
of the sag in my brow, the creases around my eyes.
There is a core of fear inside me.

I am on my own on this latest stretch
as my fellow pilgrims moved ahead.
I reset my bag and the St. James's scallop clinks.

Shrine

The fir trees cast a shadow.
The dry road passes by.
Piles of stones lie on the side of the path,
some with shoes on them,
others have ribbons around them,
or pebbles to decorate.

The place is littered with cones, wrappings from food.
There is a photo of a man in his thirties,
a note addressed to some long-lost love.

I wonder who put this together.
Is it a place where people realise their excess
then choose to walk lighter?
The wind blows and blows, gives no answer.

The River

Water flows over the stepping stones
clearing away the mud left by my boots.

I watch the brown swirl on the glassy flow
and hope my own hurt goes down the stream.

I offer up each memory as it bubbles out
while the beating heats up in my head

and my throat is dry. I cannot speak.
I am a child again, finding my words.

Silent Friend

Brown stones roll down the steep hill
when touched by my foot. I blow in and out
catching my breath. I pass by a man in hiking gear,
covered in sweat under his large backpack.
I can feel his weight. Since I have no words,
I lift a baby finger from my hiking pole and he nods to me.

Bendición

May the clouds come between you and the sun.
May the path stay dry and solid.
May the walk spare you blisters.
May the bag on your back be easy to carry.
May the shops open on time.
May the wine and beer be reasonable.
May the locals stay friendly.
May the showers in the *albergues* work.
May the snorers find another room.
May the rains come during the night.

Forest Hike

The sky is a black skin
stretched over the forest. I walk over the gravel
with a tart clicking sound, smell the eucalyptus trees.

The wind blows cold.
A jackdaw voice in my head repeats the same old fears
that I am alone and always will be.

I come across a pile of stones
shaped like a heart with words 'I love you', 'Keep going',
'*Buen Camino*', 'Take one step at a time'.

I place my hand on my heart.
The unnameable flame ushers through my body
and this keeps me going over the mucky path.

The forest is still dark
and soon the gaps thin the trees out.
I step onto a bright open field.

Footprints

Water spills down a bank
and makes this path mucky.
Footprints mark the way.

I avoid walking over them
as each is special in its own shape.
I imagine who created the print:

A middle-aged woman in an orange coat
hobbles over the path. She does ten kilometres
a day, rubs her feet in a village.

A gang of shirtless male teenagers,
treading the ground without concern.
They sing to kill the boredom.

An old man keeps secret – six months left to live.
He wishes to make it to Santiago
and wants to meet as many people as he can.

I cannot avoid
leaving a trail from my own shoes and poles
like some fierce four-footed animal.

Touching Skin

I was embarrassed by stripping in front of this physio.
She could see the carpet of my hairy chest and back.
My belly flopped out. I tried to keep it in.
At first, the pressure was a shock. She pressed my skin
like kneading dough and her touch was a little rough.
She massaged the leg muscles and then the feet.
'Turn over' she said, first in Spanish, then in English.
My skin was smoothed and freshened.
Warmth suffused my body, my nerves tingled.
I came from the plinth, remade.

Sunlight reflected on ...

different-sized stones
scattered on the drying path –
distant memory

copious droplets
from the high-speed sprinkler –
rainbow in the flow

beige and brown corn stalks
stretch to the far off mountains –
shimmer of Spanish heat

the sand-covered path –
making our way on this route
this beetle and I

the eyes of a pilgrim
I have not seen in days –
our two bags resting

my dipped sore feet –
I release this long journey
into the stream

Mariposas

for Arlene Fox

Around and over the path
are ten butterflies.

Delicate powdered wings,
blue, white and black.

They flutter towards me and away
and once nearly into my mouth.

A fellow walker tells me they are souls
that choose to stay behind.

She said in the Gross-Rosen camp there were
hundreds resting on the walls of the huts.

I count the butterflies that come across my path
during the rest of that day and I lose count.

Warm Bedrock

I lie on a slab of black rock.
Heat emits from deep within the Earth's core.

The sun burnishes the landscape.
Rocks absorb the light willingly –
a slow child careful with what it picks up and plays with.

A lizard pads its way across the rock
with a fly in its mouth, crunching with care.
The lizard looks at me, wondering what creature I am.

The skin on the back of my legs heats up
and the sun lingers. I should make more progress
but I want to while away the day here.

Thunderstorm Coming

The horse chestnut trees cover
the way, shading off the sunlight.
The mud flows down this rocky path.
The air is tight with the threat of thunder.
I am covered in sweat from the dead heat
as I wish I could replace my bleeding feet
with a new pair free from any pain
to get me over this rough terrain.
Memories come that are not tender.
I have reached the point of surrender
and I seek forgiveness for my sins,
forgive everyone for their deeds.
Dying to my old life, living this death,
God, I ask for your divine breath.

Dawn over O Cebreiro

Black gives way to many colours
and the rain assaults the windows of the *albergue*.
I get up at five o'clock quietly
as I want to avoid walking with anyone.

Mist is thick and clings around here.
A row of lights shine like angels.
Wind-washed clothes are scattered
on the footpath outside the *albergue*.

I see the sea, then realise it's not the sea,
but a blanket of clouds where high peaks
come through. A yellow arrow points the way
and I am tempted to follow the wrong path.

At Cee

For the last three days
between Santiago and Cee
I have walked at a furious pace
trying to outrun my thoughts.
Now I am on the cliff edge gazing at the sea.

I abandoned my fellow pilgrims
as I felt uneasy with a disparate group
from Italy, Germany, England, Brazil and America.
I felt that they found me unacceptable,
a contract written in white ink,
its terms clear but silent.

They booked an apartment for themselves
and I was given the couch to sleep on.
I snuck off without a word and found my own bed to stay in.
I have tried to forgive myself to no avail.
Their faces haunt me.

Walking along the cliff edge
I realise I have always been on the edge
of friends, family, neighbours and work,
and I exclude myself.

The sea is a sheet of the clearest blue,
the wind brushes a ripple over the surface.

Sunset at Finisterre

The sun pinks the glowing clouds.
A red band is on the horizon
as the dome of the sky turns to ochre.

The moon comes out brighter.
I can see the creases on her face,
make out the Sea of Tranquility.

Some pilgrims are burning their clothes.
The smell of ashen cloth fills the air.
Burn my sins away, burn, burn.

The red band loses its colour.
The sky is black and makes me think:
why do I carry all of this hurt?

I look to the lighthouse for an answer.
The signal goes round and round
and keeps to its slow motion.

Notes

The title of 'At The Still Point' alludes to the line from T. S. Eliot's 'at the still point of the turning world' from *Burnt Norton*. The poems in Part II: Camino Cantos were written on the Camino de Santiago pilgrimage I did in 2016. The Camino begins in France at St. Jean Pied de Port in the Pyrenees and ends in Santiago de Compostela, Galicia, Spain. This route is called the Camino Frances as there are other Camino routes. The Camino Frances is 769 km long. A further extension of the Camino continues to Finisterre. The cover painting is *The Only Tree In The Burren* by Paul Henry.

Glossary

Albergue: a hostel.

Bendición: a blessing.

Buen Camino: a greeting which means, 'Have a good Camino.'

Cee: a town on the coast of Galicia in northern Spain.

Finisterre: this means 'land's end'. It has a well-known lighthouse.

Gross-Rosen camp: a World War II concentration camp.

Mariposas: butterflies.

O Cebreiro: a high elevation point of the Camino and an early medieval village.

St. James's Scallop: Saint James is the patron saint of the Camino. The scallop is the symbol of the Camino.

Acknowledgements

Some poems, or early versions of them, have been published in: *All to One Side* anthology by the Market Place Poetry Group, Ballyroan Library website, *Beir Bua, Blithe Spirit, Boyne Berries, Crannóg, Crossways, Cyphers, Flare, Impossible Archetype, Mustang Bally* anthology by the Ballyfermot Writer's Group and Ballymun Writer's Group, www.poetry24.co.uk, *seashores haiku journal, Teachers' Who Write* anthology by the Waterford Teachers' Centre, *The Blue Nib, The Source,* and *The Waxed Lemon.*

'Invitation' won 2nd place in the Barbara Haley Poetry Competition in 1998. 'Pass' was highly commended in the Ballyroan Library Competition in 2018. 'Driftwood' was shortlisted in the Bray Poetry Competition 2018. Eight poems were Highly Commended in the Blue Nib Chapbook Contest IV in 2018 and another eight poems were shortlisted for the Blue Nib Chapbook Contest V in 2019. Silent House was long-listed in the Over The Edge New Writer Competition 2019. 'Aftermath' won 2nd place in the Ballyroan Library Poetry Prize in 2020.

Thanks

Thanks to the editors of the above journals and anthologies who published the poems and to the judges of the various prizes that were awarded to me. Thanks to James Harpur for giving a critical reading of an early version of the Camino Cantos, to the members of the Parnell Square Writers' Group who gave feedback on the collection, and to members of the Hibernian Writers' Group who gave feedback on individual poems.

About the Author

The Singing Hollow is Diarmuid Fitzgerald's first collection of poetry. Poems not part of *The Singing Hollow* have been published in *Cyphers, Green Carnations: an LGBTQ anthology, It's a Queer City: All the Same, an anthology of LGBT Writing from Limerick,* and in *The Stinging Fly.* These will form part of the next poetry manuscript called *Rainbow Street.* Two collections of haiku were published by Alba Publishing. *Thames Way* appeared in 2015 and *A Thousand Sparks* appeared in 2018. Diarmuid won the Individual Artist Bursary 2018 from South Dublin County Council. Also in 2018, Diarmuid won a scholarship to attend the Yeats International Summer School. You can follow Diarmuid and read poems on www.deewriter. com and follow him on Instagram on @deewriters.